UNDERSTANDING INSURANCE

This No Nonsense Guide tells you how insurance works and what you need to know about:

- Life insurance
- Health insurance
- Residential and real estate insurance
- Automobile insurance
- Making a claim

THE NO NONSENSE LIBRARY
NO NONSENSE FINANCIAL GUIDES

How to Choose a Discount Stockbroker, Revised Edition
How to Finance Your Child's College Education, Revised Edition
How to Plan and Invest for Your Retirement
How to Use Credit and Credit Cards, Revised Edition
The New Tax Law and What It Means to You
Personal Banking
Understanding Common Stocks, Revised Edition
Understanding Insurance
Understanding IRAs, Revised Edition
Understanding Money Market Funds, Revised Edition
Understanding Mutual Funds, Revised Edition
Understanding Social Security
Understanding the Stock Market, Revised Edition
Understanding Stock Options and Futures Markets, Revised Edition
Understanding Tax-Exempt Bonds
*Understanding Treasury Bills and Other U.S. Government Securities,
    Revised Edition*

OTHER NO NONSENSE GUIDES:

Car Guides
Career Guides
Cooking Guides
Health Guides
Legal Guides
Parenting Guides
Photography Guides
Real Estate Guides
Study Guides
Success Guides
Wine Guides

NO NONSENSE FINANCIAL GUIDE®

UNDERSTANDING INSURANCE

Gerald Gladney

Longmeadow Press

For Kamau and Tenderness

UNDERSTANDING INSURANCE

Copyright © 1991 by Longmeadow Press

No Nonsense Financial Guide is a trademark controlled by Longmeadow Press.

ISBN 0-681-41049-3

Production services: Marie Brown Associates
Cover and inside design: Ken Brown
Editing/copyediting: Karen Taylor
Typography: ANY Phototype, Inc.

Printed in the United States of America

0 9 8 7 6 5 4 3 2 1

UNDERSTANDING INSURANCE

Contents

Part V   Other Issues

Preface

Are you a homeowner? Do you own a car? Is your primary residence an apartment? Are you dependent on your work income for survival? Are there other people dependent on you?

Can you handle the financial strain of a personal disaster? Are you adequately protected against the risks that occur daily? In other words, are you adequately insured?

In general, insurance is an apparatus designed to eliminate or reduce the economic risk to all insureds by using a system of equitable contributions out of which losses are paid. There are several types of insurance. The chances are, you are covered by one of them. It is also likely that you are more than adequately covered in some areas, and inadequately covered in others.

Understanding Insurance is a guide through the insurance maze. We discuss the main types of insurance sold: private health, property, liability, and life insurance. This book will also help you choose the right insurance company, and provide guidelines for making a claim.

PART ONE
INTRODUCTION

1

HOW INSURANCE WORKS

Insurance works on the principle of shared losses. People who wish to be insured against particular types of losses agree to make regular payments. Those regular payments are called *premiums*. The individuals paying premiums are called *policyholders*. In return, these people receive a contract. The contract is called a *policy*. The company promises to pay a certain sum of money for the types of losses stated in the policy. The amount of money paid by the insurance company to the policyholders is known as the *benefit* or the *claim*.

The insurance company uses the premiums to invest in income-producing enterprises. The company pays benefits from the premiums it collects and from investment income the premiums earn.

Insurance works because policyholders are willing to trade a small, certain loss, for the guarantee that they will be paid or *indemnified* in case of a larger loss.

Life insurance, for example, helps replace income lost to a family if a wage-earning member dies. Health insurance helps pay medical bills. Casualty insurance pays all or part of the loss if a house is destroyed by fire. Automobile insurance helps cover the cost of damages resulting from a car accident.

Risk Management

Personal risk management means preparing to deal with uncertainty in your life. This uncertainty exists because you are constantly exposed to the possibility of loss, injury, disadvantage, or destruction. As you identify each risk, you will have to determine how to treat it. Buying insurance is one way of managing risk.

Insurance companies also manage their risks by building *co-insurance* mechanisms into some of their policies. In most cases, when you seek to finance your exposure to risk with the assistance of insurance companies, you'll find that many companies will "share" your exposure to risk, rather than accept 100% of the responsibility for the loss if it should occur. The reason for this is, if you have arranged for the financing of a risk by paying a low premium, you may become less careful than you should be, and cause an insurance company to pick up 100% of the loss should a casualty occur.

Sharing risks seems to make everyone involved more careful. You will find insurance companies much more willing to pick up the major economic loss of risks that you are exposed to if you will share with them in those losses via *deductibles*, e.g., they will pay 80% of the loss, if you will pay 20%.

Insurance companies also manage their risks by screening potential policyholders to determine their insurance suitability. Private insurance companies are profit-making businesses. Their ability to make profits protects the policyholder's interest.

Private Insurance

Social Security, workman's compensation, and Medicaid are insurance programs, but they are government sponsored entities.

An effectively managed personal insurance program can provide you with assistance in economic survival, a basis for credit, protection in case of loss, and a means of increasing your ability to use your assets.

There are any number of groups that you may join in order to pool your potential risks so that, should you suffer a loss, the group will assist you in keeping economic loss to a minimum.

Using This Book

Insurance expenses can easily utilize a large portion of your budget. This book will help you spend your insurance dollars wisely. With each insurance policy discussed, there are some useful questions that you should ask. Keep in mind who you are. (The life insurance needs of a single male of 25 are not the same as the life insurance needs of a 30 year old single mother of three.) How do you earn a living? What do you own? Where do you live? With the information you have in hand, you can compare the insurance coverage you need with the insurance coverage you presently have. You will be able to implement a personal risk management program in which you buy insurance when you should, don't buy insurance when you shouldn't, and have cost-effective benefits in force when you need them.

There are some other things you should keep in mind when designing your risk management program. Consider the self-insurance option. *Self-insurance* means setting aside funds to meet possible losses or paying for your losses out of pocket. Consider raising your deductible (a modified form of self-insurance). Look for insurance bargains. One important thing to do is to periodically reassess your policies. As you change, your insurance needs change. It is wise to make sure your policies meet your evolving needs.

2

HOW THE INSURANCE INDUSTRY IS REGULATED

The insurance industry has long had powerful lobbies. In 1945, the industry mobilized Congressional support to pass the McCarran-Ferguson Act. Under this act, the Federal government was prohibited from overseeing the insurance industry. Regulation does take place, but it takes place at the state level. There are differences, though, in the quality and regulations throughout the states. New York State's insurance commission has about 800 employees and is generally regarded as the best of state regulators. But there are some state regulatory departments with less than half a dozen employees.

If an insurance company is licensed to do business in a particular state, you may assume that the state insurance department has examined the company and its portfolio or products and found them to be in compliance with state regulations. This level of protection, though, isn't always reliable. Even in New York, insurance commissioners do not have the authority to tell insurance companies how to run their businesses.

The state does collect information about companies doing business within its jurisdiction that can be of value. If you request it, information that a company provides to the state regulators is available to you.

State Guarantee Systems

There are 39 states in the U.S. that have guaranteed funds for insurance. When an insurer becomes insolvent, the insurance companies doing business in the state are responsible for paying off claims. The insurance companies operating in the state contribute to a fund that is drawn on to pay the claims of the failed insurance companies. But because there is no uniform standard, many of the state funds don't have adequate reserves.

Private Rating Services

There are several private industry-rating services that monitor the insurance industry. The oldest is A.M. Best Company of New Jersey. They have been rating insurers since 1899. Best provides information regarding an insurance company's financial condition, a synopsis of its history, information on its management, operating commitments, and the states in which it may underwrite insurance. The Best Company also grants its own ratings to insurance companies, that assess strengths and weaknesses in four areas: underwriting, expense control, reserve adequacy, and investments. Ratings range from A+ (superior) to C (fair). A.M. Best reports are usually available at your local library. They publish a Life/Health annual and a Property/Casualty annual. The new edition of the annual is usually available in June. They also publish a monthly newsletter which updates the annual.

Standard & Poor's has a service which rates a very limited number of companies on their claim-paying ability. Standard & Poor's is hired by the insurance company to do an evaluation of their business operations. Standard & Poor's ratings range from AAA (extremely strong capacity to meet contractual policy obligations) to D (default, terms of the obligation will not be met). While Standard & Poor's guarantees the integrity of their reports, the reports are only available to the public at the discretion of the insurance company. If the insurance company doesn't like the report they can suppress it.

Moody's Investor Service of New York rates the quality of a company's investment portfolio. They are another highly regarded rating service. But as with Standard & Poor's, their reports are available at the discretion of the insurance company.

Insurance Forum

Insurance Forum is a monthly newsletter published by Dr. Joseph M. Belth of Indiana University. Dr. Belth has been referred to as the Ralph Nader of the insurance industry. He publishes a list of insurance companies that have received top ratings from Best Company for the last ten consecutive years. You may request his most current list by writing to the *Insurance Forum*, P.O. Box 245, Ellettsville, Indiana 47429. Include a stamped, self-addressed envelope with your request.

BEST RATING CLASSIFICATIONS

The following is an explanation of the classifications A.M. Best assigns to the insurance companies they review. The Best company rates 1500 life and health insurers and 2300 property-casualty firms, annually. The Best rating classifications have three general categories: primary, modifiers, and not assigned.

Primary Classifications

A+ — Superior   B   — Good
A   — Excellent   C+ — Fairly Good
B+ — Very Good   C   — Fair

Modifiers

Modifiers are classifications that are assigned to some insurers that receive the A+ to C rating. They appear in lower-case letters after the primary classification.

"c" — *Contingent Rating*. Temporarily assigned to a company when there has been a decline in performance in its profitability, leverage, and/or liquidity results, but the decline has not been significant enough to warrant an immediate reduction in the company's primary rating.

"e" — *Parent Rating*. Indicates a company which meets Best's minimum size requirements and is a wholly-owned subsidiary of a rated insurer; however, it has not accumulated at least five consecutive years of operating for rating purposes.

"p" — *Pooled Rating.* Assigned to companies under common management or ownership which pool 100% of their net business. All members participating in the pooling arrangement will be assigned the same rating and financial size category based on the consolidated performance of the group.

"r" — *Reinsured Rating.* Indicates that the rating and financial size category assigned to the company is that of an affiliated carrier which reinsures 100% of the company's business.

Not Assigned Classifications

Companies not receiving the Best primary rating are given "Not Assigned" classifications which are divided into ten different categories to identify the various reasons the company was not assigned a primary rating.

NA 1 *Inactive* — Assigned to a company which has no net insurance business in force, or is virtually dormant and is not 100% reinsured by another company.

NA 2 *Less Than Minimum Size* — Assigned to a company whose annual net premiums written do not meet the minimum size requirement of $1,000,000.

NA 3 *Insufficient Experience* — Assigned to a company which meets the minimum size requirement, but has not accumulated at least five consecutive years of representative operating experience.

NA 4 *Rating Procedure Inapplicable* — Assigned to a company when the nature of its business and/or operations are such that Best's normal rating procedure for insurers do not properly apply.

NA 5 *Significant Change* — Assigned to a previously rated company whose representative operating experience has been, or is expected to be, significantly interrupted or changed.

NA 6 *Reinsured by Unrated Reinsurer* — Assigned to a company which has reinsured a substantial portion of its business with reinsurers who have not been assigned a Best's rating.

NA 7 *Below Minimum Standards* — Assigned to a company that meets minimum size and experience requirements, but does not meet the minimum standards for a Best's rating of "C."

NA 8 *Incomplete Financial Information*—Assigned to a company which fails to submit, prior to the rating deadline, complete financial information for any year in the current five-year period under review.

NA 9 *Company Request*—Assigned when a company is eligible for a rating but disputes the Best's rating assignment or procedure.

NA 10 *Under State Supervision* — Assigned when a company is under conservatorship, rehabilitation, receivership, or any other form of supervision, control, or restraint by state regulatory authorities.

3

CHOOSING THE RIGHT
REPRESENTATIVES

Choosing an insurance agent or company is not an exact science, but there are some serviceable guidelines. A number of experts suggest that you use the Best Company and *Insurance Forum* rating reports in order to select an insurance company. You are advised to buy insurance from companies that have been rated A or above for a prolonged period of time.

Insurance is sold either on a direct basis via the media or through a general agency system. If you are using an agent, it is wise to look for certification such as CLU for chartered life underwriter, ChFC for chartered financial planner, or LIA for licensed insurance adviser. An agent must be licensed to sell or offer insurance products in any particular state. In order for the agent to possess a specific license, he or she must pass an examination. Agents must conform to state law when selling new life insurance policies, and when making recommendations about the replacement of existing life insurance.

Because state regulations vary, and because regulations are, frequently, in the best interest of the insurer, you are advised to follow these additional recommendations for choosing an insurance agent.

- Get a recommendation from someone whose judgment you trust.

- When reading articles about insurance, look for names of people in your area who are favorably written about or quoted by their peers.

- Ask direct questions of the insurance professional you are considering, regarding his or her background, experience, and references.

- And look for evidence of how the person keeps abreast of current information in the field.

These general standards will not only help you in selecting an insurance professional, they will enable you to better understand the agent you choose. You need an agent who will make recommendations based on your way of thinking, your financial philosophy, and your immediate- and long-range financial requirements.

PART TWO
LIFE INSURANCE

4

TERM INSURANCE

All life insurance has two common costs—the charges for mortality and expenses. The money paid into a policy is applied to these two costs with any excess held in reserve. If you pay in more than is required for the current year's mortality and expense charges, the surplus is invested for you in an investment account within the policy.

Expense charges are incurred in issuing and managing the policy. Mortality charges or life insurance costs are calculated by the insurance company to cover the amount of life insurance promised your beneficiary. The insurance company, in effect, has pooled you with others of the same age, sex, smoking habits, and physical makeup. If enough people are pooled together, the number who will die, in any one year, from this large group, can be predicted with great statistical accuracy.

Mortality and expense costs are a part of every life insurance policy. They cannot be avoided or the insurance company would go out of business. The amount allocated to investment, within the insurance policy, will be discussed in Chapter 5 on Cash-Value Insurance.

Term insurance requires the payment of the mortality and expense charges, and nothing more. Typically, the most efficient form of term insurance is yearly renewable and convertible term. With this policy, you pay the mortality and expense charges for the current year only, and you accept the fact that as you get older, your mortality costs will go up. In each succeeding year, you can expect the premium on this type of policy to increase.

If you want very inexpensive term insurance, don't ask the insurance company to do anything more than pay the death benefit. As a result of not having to make any extra promises, the insurance company will be able to minimize your cost. If, however, you want more from the insurance company, such as the promise to accept your premium in the coming years, and to allow your insurance to continue (renewable term insurance), you will have to pay a little bit extra for the promise of renewability. Most people willingly pay extra for this renewal privilege because they never know when they may go from "insurable" to "uninsurable." Uninsurability may be a result of the deterioration of one's health, latest avocation, or current occupation. In any case, insurance companies may not wish to provide new life insurance at any cost. At that time, the renewal privilege on existing policies will become particularly important.

The convertibility feature in a term life insurance policy allows you to change it into any of the other types of contracts that are offered by the same company that issued your term insurance policy. However, if you are dealing with an insurance company that has an incomplete portfolio of products, or does not have the type of product you'd want to replace your term insurance, the convertibility feature is of no value to you.

There also are term insurance policies which charge a level premium for five years, ten years, even as long as twenty years. To accomplish this, the insurer takes a look at the yearly renewable and convertible term rate required each year and averages it out over a specific time period.

They then ask you for an average level premium for the five-, ten-, or twenty-year period.

The disadvantage of this type of policy is that you are paying more than is required in the early years so that you may pay less than is normally required in the future. If you keep the term insurance policy for the total period of time it might be a fair arrangement; however, when the time value of money is taken into consideration, it usually works to the insurance company's benefit. Also, since many people adjust their term insurance policies from year to year, paying this additional premium at the outset, when you may not own the policy for its duration, can be a waste of money.

You also can buy a term life insurance policy with a level premium, but the death benefit will be reduced each year so that your premium is sufficient to cover the mortality and expense charges that exist during that particular year. This is commonly referred to as *decreasing term insurance.*

The insurance companies like to market it as mortgage insurance to make you feel as if you need to buy it. This type of coverage allows the insurance company to reduce your death benefit each year. To avoid this, you could buy a level, yearly renewable and convertible insurance policy and then, in the coming years, if you decide that you do not need that amount of life insurance, you can ask the insurer to reduce the face amount. Term insurance is never paid up. You are only covered for the time designated by your premium. When you stop paying, coverage ends.

5

CASH-VALUE LIFE INSURANCE

Cash-value life insurance contains the two basic elements of term insurance—mortality and expense charges—and adds to them an investment element that offers the policyholder some cash advantages. Cash-value life insurance includes whole life, universal life, variable life, and universal variable life insurance. In these types of insurances, the policyholder pays additional money that earns a return that is applied to your policy. These policies differ in how the investment components are managed and in how interest is earned by the investment.

Whole Life

Whole life insurance is a policy that has, within it, charges for expenses and mortality and additional funds which are invested into the long-term bond and mortgage portfolio of the insurance company. It is a policy which has a fixed premium and a fixed face amount.

Prior to 1976, all life insurance policies issued by companies in the United States invested the appropriate funds in the general portfolio of the company. The long-term general portfolio of life insurance companies is comprised primarily of long-term bonds and mortgages. The fixed-interest rate, long-term bonds and mortgages within this investment portfolio earned the prevailing interest rate at the time they were purchased. It was this type of fixed-interest portfolio that was exposed to the incredible, rapid increases in interest rates that brought the prime rate up to 21½% by December of 1980. In that environment, a mortgage note or a long-term bond with a 5%, 6%, 7%, or 8% interest rate decreased in value as other investment interest rates went up. Who wanted to earn 5% when they could suddenly get 15%? It was at this point that the Federal Trade Commission chose to examine insurance company investments.

Variable Life Insurance

Variable life insurance provides a guaranteed minimum death benefit, but the actual benefit paid may be more depending on the market value of investments within the contract at the time of the insured's death. The investment vehicles available, within this policy, are provided by common-stock holdings and money market accounts; the policy owner can choose either investment option, and change back and forth between the two. Like whole-life, this policy has a fixed premium and a fixed face amount. If you fail to pay the premiums when due, the policy will lapse. Value that has accrued in the policy will revert to a fixed life policy or default into, what is referred to as, paid-up extended term insurance. Here, the value of the policy is used for buying term insurance for whatever period of time the cash available will sustain.

Universal Life

Universal life insurance, first introduced in late 1979, was the life insurance industry's direct response to the demands of the consumer for the high interest rates of the time. The insurance companies promised the policyholder a specified rate of interest for a one-year period. Where variable life had a fixed minimum face amount and fixed premium, it gave the policyholder flexibility of investment; universal life eliminated the fixed premium and face amount and offered no flexibility of investment.

The universal life policyholder can manipulate the face amount to increase or decrease the death benefit in accordance with his or her life situation. The policy owner also has flexibility in paying premiums. He can add to the investment by increasing premium payments, or decrease current investment by choosing not to pay premiums. At a minimum, the policy must have sufficient monies in it to cover the mortality and expense charges.

Universal Variable Life

This type of policy was introduced around 1985. It combined the flexibility in premium payment and face amount of universal life with the flexibility of investment offered in variable life. Universal variable life gives the policyholder a great deal of control. The policyholder can make decisions on face amount and on levels of funding within the policy. Good policy owner management can make these policies perform extremely well.

Life Insurance Riders

Life insurance policies can contain some additional benefits that come in the form of riders. The most common types of riders are: waiver of premium, yearly-renewable term insurance, one-year term insurance, cost of living, accidental death benefit, purchase option, and paid-up dividend additions.

A waiver of premium is a provision available in many life insurance policies that exempts the insured from the payment of premiums after he or she has been disabled for a specified period of time. Waiver of premium riders also exist in disability income health policies.

The yearly-renewable term rider is also mentioned in Chapter 4. It can be added to most term plans. The rider provides level term insurance for a period of one year and is renewed at the end of each year without medical examination. The rider can also be converted to some non-term plans without evidence of insurability. This rider should be used when you cannot afford the amount of life insurance you need on a non-term basis. The length of time the rider can remain in force, as a rider, depends on the specific company.

A one-year term insurance rider is used when you wish your death benefit to increase by the amount of the reserve. On each dividend date, one-year term insurance equal to the cash value is purchased. This rider is paid from dividends. This rider is used when it is impossible for you to purchase the insurance you need.

The cost of living rider, which is also paid from dividends, provides one-year term insurance coverage which will be adjusted, each year, in accordance with changes in the cost of living as measured by the consumer price index. There may be limitations on additional coverage to be purchased. The amount of insurance is unknown. It should be used when you have calculated your insurance on a real dollar basis and cannot afford to purchase the required amount.

The accidental death benefit is generally referred to as "double indemnity." You should consult with each company for its complete definition. Briefly, such a definition should state that the benefit is payble if you die within 120 days from the date of an accidental bodily injury as a result of the injury. In this case, the death benefit payable to your beneficiary will double.

The purchase option rider enables you to purchase additional life insurance, without proof of insurability and usually at specific times. Check with the individual insurance companies for the specified terms.

The paid-up dividend additions rider is used to purchase additional paid-up life insurance. The paid-up amount of insurance has its own cash value. The rider is used to provide flexibility for a traditional whole life premium life policy.

A Consumer Note About Cash Value Life Insurance

A number of prominent financial advisers and commentators on the insurance industry are less than complimentary about cash-value life insurance. People such as Charles Givens, author of the best selling *Wealth Without Risk*, and insurance expert, Arthur Milton, call any life insurance other than term a rip-off.

They feel that life insurance should only be used to guard the economic safety of your family for as long as you have family members dependent upon you. It is, in their opinion, a woefully inadequate method of accumulating cash value. The cash value of your non-term life insurance is not added to the face amount of your insurance policy when you die. If you withdraw your cash from your policy before death, your beneficiary will receive the face amount less the amount of cash you withdrew.

Critics also note that insurance salesmen earn a greater commission for the sale of cash-value life insurance policies than term life insurance.

Finally, if you fulfill the terms of your cash-value policies, someone will collect.

STOCK VERSUS MUTUAL COMPANY

Your cash-value policy may be issued by a stock insurance company as opposed to a mutual insurance company. The difference between the two is that a stock company is owned by its stockholders, and favorable investment returns, favorable expense experience, and lower mortality experience benefit the stockholders. Conversely, in a mutual insurance company, which is owned by the policyholders, these gains are passed through by way of dividends. The premiums for stock company cash-value policies are usually lower than the premiums for an equal amount of insurance with a mutual insurance company.

In the 1980's, mutual company policies became more popular because there were considerable increases in investment returns and those earnings are passed on to the policyholders.

You should also note that mutual companies are limited to borrowing when they need to raise additional cash. A stock company can raise cash by selling more shares. The debt burden of an insurer can, sometimes, adversely effect your expense.

6

INSURANCE WITH LIVING BENEFITS

Annuities

As you know, the three basic elements of a life insurance policy are the expenses, mortality charges, and, when applicable, the investment account. The investment account of an annuity contract is unique in that it can grow without current taxation. It also includes a charge for expenses. It does not have significant mortality charges. Many variable annuities do include a mortality charge which provides that, in the event of the annuitant's death, the beneficiary will receive either the investment in the contract or the annuity's account value, whichever is greater. This provides death protection in case of poor investment results. Other than this minor safety feature, annuity contracts are oriented to benefit the purchaser rather than the beneficiary.

The primary objective of the annuity contract is to pay investment returns to the annuitant. Annuities are useful

27

to accumulate money for some future date, usually in retirement, or to provide for the systematic payment of funds that have accumulated.

The annuity contract loses all of its tax-deferral if it has not been used up prior to the annuitant's death. It can be passed to a beneficiary, but any income tax liabilities in the contract go with it and become income tax liabilities for the beneficiary of the contract.

The term annuity is defined as an amount of money payable yearly or at other regular intervals, for a certain or uncertain period. It is a life insurance policy with living benefits.

Endowment Policies

Endowment policies are another way of receiving living benefits from life insurance. Endowment policies are often used to pay college costs or to meet some other major financial goal. At the end of a prescribed period, which is usually 10, 15, 20, or 30 years, the face value of the policy is paid to the owner. Mortality charges are higher in endowment policies than in annuity contracts because if, you die before the payment term is up, your beneficiary will receive the full face value.

7

DETERMINING YOUR LIFE INSURANCE NEEDS

Life insurance is insurance company money to be received by a beneficiary upon the death of the insured. The objective of life insurance is to make sure that those important to you will not suffer undue financial hardship as a result of your death.

Determining the amount of life insurance you want for your beneficiary, in a family situation, is an extremely personal decision.

How Much Life Insurance

How much life insurance you need is based upon your requirements. What do you own? What are the economic needs of the people who are dependent upon you? Do the needs of your dependents include education costs? What are your debts? What are your income tax liabilities? What will your funeral costs be? Your answers to these questions will determine the dollar amount your beneficiary would need in order to live in the manner he/she is accustomed to.

Protecting Your Family

After you have chosen a quality insurer, most insurance advisers suggest the purchase of a term life insurance policy with a yearly renewable rider and a convertible provision. This means that you will pay the insurance company the amount necessary to pay the mortality and expenses on a policy in the amount you've determined is necessary for a one-year period. This type of policy allows you to spend the minimum amount to put a policy in force, immediately, and protect your family as quickly as possible. You may have opportunities to obtain such life insurance through your employer, via group insurance, or through some organization that you belong to with association group life insurance.

Getting your policy in force as quickly as possible will not only remove a financial burden from your family, it will also prepare you for making additional decisions. You will know how much it costs to own life insurance. You will know the mortality and expense charges required as a result of your age, sex, smoking habit, general health condition, and maybe even your occupation. Once this minimum cost has been determined and accepted by you, decisions can be made as to how to finance the payment of these mortality and expense charges. Your decision concerning how to finance the payment of your mortality and expense charges should be based upon the kind of life insurance you want, the availability of funds, and your investment opportunities and objectives.

PART THREE
HEALTH INSURANCE

8

MEDICAL EXPENSE HEALTH INSURANCE

Health insurance is costly. The objective of medical expense insurance is to make sure that you and your family are never exposed to medical bankruptcy. With this objective in mind, the first requirement for a policy should be that it has an unlimited maximum. This is not always possible although, between 1980 and 1988, it was more readily available. A number of major insurance companies no longer offer unlimited policies. They have reduced their maximums to $1 million. Although the $1 million maximum sounds like a significant amount, and it certainly is, that does not mean it is necessarily enough. Your strategy should be to go for the best, request the unlimited, and compromise only if you find that the best is unavailable or impractical.

Optimally, after you have paid an acceptable deductible, the policy should cover all physician-prescribed treatments to diagnose and correct a medical condition. Deductibles are a relatively small percentage of your health-care costs, such as 20%; the insurance company pays the other

80%. It is entirely possible that you could go medically bankrupt paying 20% of unlimited bills.

For extra protection, you will want to purchase what is referred to as a "stop-loss provision" in order to obligate the insurance company to pay 100% of the medical bills for the balance of the calendar year. This serves to limit your out-of-pocket costs during any one calendar year, which is the key to avoiding medical bankruptcy. When choosing health insurance look for an unlimited maximum, comprehensive coverage, reasonable deductibles, and an acceptable stop-loss.

Pre-existing Conditions

Pre-existing conditions may be an obstacle you will have to face. When applying for individual insurance, as opposed to group insurance, you will have to answer questions regarding your medical history. On other policies, such as group insurance, you may not have to respond to any medical questions, but the policy may state that it will not pay benefits for conditions that manifested themselves before the policy was put in force.

Pre-existing conditions may be excluded entirely or for certain periods of time. In certain cases, insurance companies will pay some benefits for pre-existing conditions but limit the amount of total payments. Any condition that has been diagnosed by a physician should be revealed on the application because if you file a claim for an unrevealed pre-existing condition, the insurance company may refuse to pay.

Many policies contain limitations that restrict the benefits payable for a number of conditions. Limits on benefits paid for mental or nervous disorders, and drug and alcohol problems, are common. Insurance companies have found that bills for these types of problems frequently are unending. You will want to check any benefit restrictions carefully with your insurance professional so that your policy does not present you with any unpleasant surprises.

Medical insurance plans are usually one of four types: indemnity plans, service provider plans, preferred provider plans, or Health Maintenance Organizations.

Indemnity Plans

After you have experienced a loss, indemnity plans reimburse you for that particular loss according to the policy provisions. Indemnity plans offer the insured the advantage of selecting his or her own physician and/or hospital. You may choose the best, and the best may also be the most expensive — this has been the problem with the indemnity plans. The giver of care and the receiver of care have no personal incentive to keep costs reasonable. Consequently, costs have gotten out of hand. Recent medical insurance plans have been designed to involve both the recipient and the care-giver in providing cost-efficient medical care and, in this way, to lower the costs for all.

Service Provider Plans

This is a "fee for service" program when the insuring organization is also the provider of care. Blue Cross/Blue Shield is the first and best-known organization of this type. These "fee for service" organizations provide their participants with the facilities of member hospitals and physicians, for a monthly subscriber's fee. If the insurance company and the provider are one and the same, the insurance company maintains cost control. Theoretically, this makes service provider plans more able to estimate the charge to subscribers.

Preferred Provider Plans

Preferred provider plans are arrangements established by commercial insurance companies following the

Blue Cross/Blue Shield example. Coalitions of insurance companies negotiate with providers to obtain discounted rates for the insureds, and then guarantee patients to those providers. The benefits of using these providers are lower deductibles, lower co-insurance, and, in some cases, less paperwork as opposed to using a provider outside of the network.

Health Maintenance Organizations

Health Maintenance Organizations are assemblages of physicians and hospitals joined together in one business arrangement. The HMO promises that they will maintain their members' health for a monthly fee.

All of these arrangements work well if they are economically sound and if you are in fairly good health. However, if either of these factors deteriorate, the whole system may deteriorate. In 1989, a major HMO filed for Chapter 11 bankruptcy protection, leaving hundreds of thousands of people in doubt about their coverage.

Private Industry

How good are private insurance companies at managing health care? In the preferred provider organization, your health-care is supervised by what is called a "gate-keeper" or "quarterback" doctor. All basic medical services will be delivered by this physician. If you need a specialist, this gatekeeper will assign that specialist; and if that specialist wants to take an X-ray, she will ask permission of your gatekeeper. This health-care concept is just developing and will take more time and patience before it will work well.

One alternative offered by many commercial insurance companies is the combination indemnity plan/PPO option. Under this arrangement, the insured employee does not commit to indemnity or PPO in advance, but decides which to use when care is needed. The employer will attempt to steer the employee toward the PPO by means of lower deductibles and lower co-insurance than are available under the indemnity plan, but it is ultimately the employee's choice.

Individual Medical Insurance

If employer provided health insurance is not a viable alternative, you can directly apply to an insurance company for an individually issued policy. The advantage of this procedure is that you can, more or less, dictate the type of benefits you want. The disadvantage is that you have no employer to help you defray the expense. Unfortunately, individual insurance is most readily available if you are healthy. In applying for an individual health insurance policy, the insurance company will ask you a dizzying array of medical questions. They will want to know the health history of you and everyone in your family. It is in your best interest to divulge everything because even if you have a particular health condition that the insurance company might not wish to cover, they may be able to issue the policy with an exclusion rider.

The policy would cover everything but that particular condition, which is certainly a better alternative than no health insurance at all. Another advantage of an individual policy is the availability of a guaranteed-renewable contract, which prohibits the insurance company from cancelling your policy but allows it to adjust the costs for the insurance as long as it does so for all individuals in the same risk category. Many people opt to purchase an individually issued, guaranteed-renewable health insurance policy to gain more control over the continuation of their personal health insurance.

Choosing a high deductible can keep the cost down, and the guaranteed renewability assures them that they can keep the policy in force as long as they want to pay the billed premiums.

Association Medical Insurance

Another alternative for obtaining medical insurance may be through an association of which you are a member. Many such organizations provide their members with various forms of insurance. Some of the organizations sell the insurance just to provide an extra benefit for their membership; others, in order to make a profit for their organization. You, obviously, would prefer the former. What you seek, of course, is high-quality, affordable, comprehensive coverage.

Federal Government Provided Medical Insurance

Government is the final source of medical coverage. Both Federal and state governments provide medical insurance benefits. The Medicare program of the Federal government provides mandatory basic hospitalization benefits for most U.S. citizens over the age of 65, and some other special classes of individuals. This coverage, referred to as Part A, is supplemented by Part B of Medicare which is a voluntary program that provides for the payment of doctor bills. All eligible individuals should sign up for these plans three months prior to their 65th birthday. These plans are normally insufficient by themselves, and it is recommended that a supplemental plan be purchased.

Medical Supplement Insurance — Medigap

The primary reason for a Medigap policy is the need for coverage for that portion of the doctor bill that Medicare deems "excessive." In 1989, it was reported that excess charges averaged 37% more than Medicare allowable charges. You pay all of the excess. A doctor who accepts only what Medicare allows is a "participating" physician; others are "non-participating" physicians. About one out of every three physicians are participating, but this number is likely to fall due to extensive Medicare cutbacks and restrictions.

You can obtain a good Medigap policy for less than $90 per month. You should be able to locate one by consulting your local insurance professional.

State Government Insurance

Frequently, the state also offers insurance benefits via Medicaid that provide medical benefits to the indigent. The state of Illinois Medicaid pays the hospital only $.62 for every dollar the Medicaid system is billed, leaving the providers holding the bag for the rest, which was over $1 billion in 1988.

A number of states have started catastrophic medical expense pools to provide insurance benefits for those uninsurable citizens who cannot get insurance in any other way. In order to find out about state insurance pools, contact your state insurance department and ask them to send you complete information and enrollment materials. The existence and adequacy of such plans depends upon the economic health of the state in which you are a resident.

The availability of medical insurance varies a great deal from location to location. It is constantly changing. It is strongly recommended that you work with a local insurance professional as you seek to obtain and evaluate adequate medical insurance. She will know where quality coverage can be obtained for you.

AIDS

In addition to being a devastating condition, AIDS has had a significant impact on the insurance industry. Life insurance policyholders are dying sooner than the actuarial charts predict, and health insurance insurees are making more medical and disability claims. A development like this worries the industry; its instinctive response is to cut those kinds of losses.

As you know, insurance candidates are screened and high-risk applicants are usually avoided or slapped with high premiums. Once an insurer underwrites your policy, they are not above cancelling it if you fall into a high-risk category. The key to protecting yourself in this situation is knowing your policy provisions and your obligations. If your policy is cancelled unjustly, you can file a grievance with your state regulatory commission.

The insurance industry is screening applicants with subtle and overt questions about AIDS. For example, a recent application for group term life insurance from INA Life Insurance Company of New York asks, "Have you ever been treated or diagnosed by a member of the medical profession for Acquired Immune Deficiency Syndrome (AIDS), AIDS-Related Complex (ARC) or any other disorder of the immune system?" If you answer yes to that question, your application will probably be declined. If you answer no, and you make an AIDS-related claim, the insurer has cause to deny your claim and cancel your policy immediately.

The last word hasn't been written on this matter. The insurance industry might consider addressing this problem in the manner they handle other high-risk insurance situations such as the shared-risk program for high-risk drivers, and the Federal guarantee program for flood victims.

9

DISABILITY INSURANCE

Disability income insurance pays part of your income when you can't work because of accident or illness. Everyone who depends on income from a job should have disability insurance of some form.

Government Disability Plans

Although it is true that Social Security will provide benefits for disabled workers, it has been reported that 75% of all individual disability claims to Social Security are being denied. Social Security is using a definition of disability based on what are referred to as daily work activities or the Social Security acronym, DWAs. The DWAs are "standing, walking, sitting, lifting, pushing, pulling, reaching, carrying, understanding and carrying out and remembering simple instructions." Your ability to do any of these daily work activities can result in your claim for disability benefits being denied. Social Security defines disability "as an inability to engage in any substantial gainful activity by reason of any medically

41

determinable physical or mental impairment that can be expected to result in death or which has lasted or can be expected to last for a continuous period of not less than twelve months."

What about state mandated worker's compensation laws that impose absolute liability on an employer for certain injuries suffered by employees in the course of their work? Won't they provide for you? If you are not disabled on the job you will receive no benefits at all. Also, consider the adequacy of amount and duration of worker's compensation payments. In most states, benefits are inadequate in amount and duration to provide for your real needs.

If you live in California, Hawaii, New Jersey, New York, Rhode Island, or Puerto Rico, you probably have access to a state-sponsored, compulsory, temporary disability plan that is designed to provide income to disabled workers from "non-occupational" causes. These programs provide a base of benefits upon which you can build; however, they are insufficient to provide for all of your personal disability income needs.

Association Disability Insurance

You may be a member of an organization or association that offers group disability income benefits to its membership. Some of these plans are very enticing because of their low cost, but beware. These plans are sometimes inadequate because they have weak definitions of disability. You would not be considered disabled even if the only thing you could possibly do was sell pencils on the street corner. In addition, many offer benefits only in the event of an accident and/or only for a very limited period of time. Also, you do not control what happens to such a plan. If the insurance provider for your organization decides to terminate the offer of this plan, it may be cancelled. You may then find yourself trying to replace the benefits at what could be a very inopportune time. You may actually be disabled or in ill health. No one else will insure you and you will not be able to replace the benefits.

Employer-Provided Disability Insurance

Generally, employers also offer group disability income insurance plans. Just as in the association plans, it will be important for you to check the benefits provided by the plan, both for duration and quality.

The advantage of employer-provided group disability insurance is its low cost. With employer-provided plans, you do have the employer, as an advocate, to deal with the insurance company. He is interested in making sure that you have sufficient coverage and that it is the highest quality coverage obtainable. However, neither you nor your employer controls the insurance company's choice whether to continue to offer coverage or not. If the insurance company finds that providing benefits for your employer has become economically unfeasible, that insurance carrier may well decide to cancel that coverage. This lack of personal control is the primary disadvantage of employer-provided, group disability income insurance. Additionally, there may be restrictions regarding the amounts and durations of benefits, the definition of disability, the integration of the benefits provided by the plan with those provided by Social Security and/or any other source of disability income. The bottom line is that these government, association, and employer-sponsored coverages do not give you sufficient control over your benefits.

Individually Owned Disability Insurance

The most desirable disability income insurance is an individually owned policy that states that the contract may not be cancelled during your entire working life, and furthermore stipulates that the insurance company may never, during that period of time, charge you any more than is specified in the policy on the date the policy is issued. This is referred to as non-cancelable and guaranteed renewable coverage.

The policy should be of the highest quality available. It should define disability as being unable to perform, as required, within your own occupation. That definition of disability should insure you for as long as possible — preferably for life.

Accident And/Or Sickness Benefits

Some policies stipulate that benefits will be payable for life if the insured is disabled as a result of an accident, or for only two years if the disability is caused by sickness. Such policies are inadequate and should not be accepted unless nothing better may be obtained. Your policy should state that benefits will be payable for as long as possible, regardless of what has caused your disability, illness, or accident.

How Long Should Benefits Be Payable?

The benefits should last for a lifetime. If you can't get that, get the best that the insuring company offers. You don't want benefits that will terminate in the middle of a prolonged disability.

How Soon Should Benefits Begin?

Insurers can issue policies that will begin your disability benefits the moment you are disabled, but they can be very expensive. If you want to reduce the cost of your policy, you could allow the insurance company to defer benefit payments until a period of time after your disability occurs. If you can accept an elimination period of 30,60, or 90 days, you will find a substantial reduction in the amount of the premium.

Definition Of Disability

Disability may be defined as the inability of the insured, due to injury or sickness, to engage in the substantial and material duties of his or her regular occupation. Alternatively, disability may be defined as the inability of the insured to engage in any occupation. A compromise definition of disability would be the inability of the insured to engage in any occupation for which he or she is reasonably qualified, by reason of training, education, and experience.

The regular occupation definition of disability, if it is attainable, can be very expensive. You should tell the insurance company what you want then find out the best that it will offer.

The Can Do, Can't Do Period

It is preferable not to have your disability benefits end immediately after a period of total disability, because in doing so, you may jeopardize the continuation of your coverage. There is, frequently, a time during which you can do some things and cannot do others; partial disability, so to speak. You suffer partial disability if you can do only a portion of the material and substantial duties of your occupation. Therefore, a portion of your benefits should be payable, relative to the extent of your disability.

There is also something called residual disability. This type of coverage relates to your earning power. If your earning power remains the same before and after the disability, then your insurance company can discontinue your benefits. Such partial disability or residual disability provisions may not be part of your basic policy, but may be purchased as riders.

Long-Term Care Insurance

Statistics show that one person out of every four, who reaches the age of 65 will require the services of a nursing home. A solution to this problem would be to have sufficient, continually replaceable, monthly income from pensions, Social Security, and investments to adequately cover your nursing home needs. However, if you do not have such a program in place, a private nursing home insurance policy might be for you. A good policy would have a return of premium rider and no three-day hospitalization requirement. Medicaid is available as a final resort, but you must literally be without resources in order to draw on it.

PART FOUR
CASUALTY

10

REAL ESTATE

The essential purpose of real estate insurance is to give adequate coverage related to where you live and what you own.

Real Estate Liability

The law requires that people behave as reasonable and prudent individuals and, if they do not, this can constitute negligence. If that negligence leads to the injury of another individual, or the property of another individual, the negligent party may then be held liable for damages. You will be held liable for your own actions but also may be held liable for the actions of your relatives who are residents in your household. You may be held liable for the action of a resident in your household, who is under age 21, and in your care, or in the care of someone else who is a resident of your home. You may be held liable for the animals for which you are legally responsible, and also for the negligent operation of your insured, unlicensed vehicles which are used with your consent. Liability insurance

49

protects you or a member of your family from economic losses that may arise from a mistake that injures another.

You need to know how your policy will protect you from financial loss in any circumstances where you may be held responsible. Ask your insurance professional about any liability suits, where homeowner's policies were not effective in providing protection.

Real Estate Medical Payments Coverage

The medical payment provision protects you by requiring that the insurer pay all reasonable medical expenses, and funeral expenses, of persons who are injured, or killed while on your premises, with your permission (or permission from someone else who is also covered by your policy). It will also pay if someone is injured away from your premises but their injury results from your activity or from the activities of someone insured under your policy. The medical payments provision will not pay benefits to you or your other insureds. It will reimburse others for injuries related to the real estate. Make sure your policy's dollar limit for this item is realistic.

Real Property Loss

The real property clause refers to the amount your insurance carrier will pay in the event your property is totally destroyed. Your property will have to be evaluated by the insurer for several things, including a replacement estimate in the event of total loss. You will then have the option of insuring for 80% of that amount or 100%. An inflation guard endorsement provision should also be considered.

Personal Property

Personal property will only be insured if you have comprehensive, all-risk variety property insurance. You have to decide if these comprehensive riders are cost effective. It may be more feasible to self-insure any small losses that may occur.

The "HO" Puzzle

The HO stands for homeowner. When combined with a number, the HO refers to a specific type of real estate property protection. HO 1 and 2 refer to coverages for specifically identified casualties. HO 1 provided protection against fire and lightning, vandalism, malicious mischief, glass breakage, and volcanic eruption. The HO 2 policy covered the casualties of HO 1 and added six more categories: falling objects; weight of ice, snow, and sleet; heating or air conditioning system damage; water damage; frozen plumbing; and injury by artificially generated electricity. HO 1 and 2 policies still exist today but they are no longer being sold. HO 3 policies are sold today. They have an open peril or all-risk provisions. The coverage applies to the dwelling, the other structures, and loss of use. The other structures provision provides an amount of insurance equal to 10% of the amount of the dwelling itself for other detached structures on the property, such as a garage. The loss of use coverage provides funds up to 20% of the amount of coverage on the dwelling to pay any outside living expenses required as a result of the loss.

The personal property coverage of the HO 3 policy provides for payments up to an amount equal to 50% of the coverage on the dwelling to reimburse you for losses. Personal property coverage is on a broad-form, rather than an all-risk basis; this coverage for personal property may be extended by various riders.

The highest quality homeowner's policy is the HO 5. It provides all-risk coverage for the dwelling, the other structures, personal property, and loss of use. This type of policy is not always available. When it is, it can be very expensive.

Renter's/Condominium Dweller's Insurance

HO 4 policies are for renters. They provide broad-form coverage for your personal property, to the extent of 50% of your personal property coverage, and reimbursement for any loss of use of your rental property, to the extent of 20% of your personal property coverage. Renter's insurance frequently needs riders to provide adequate protection by extending and increasing the benefits of the standard HO 4 policy. This policy provides no automatic liability coverage.

HO 6 policies are for condominium owners. Condo owners are responsible for the physical repair of everything within the walls of the condominium unit; the HO 6 policy provides indemnification against any interior destruction of the unit. As with HO 4 policies, liability coverage is not automatic.

Earthquake And Flood Insurance

As you review the exclusion section of your policy, you may find some disconcerting exclusions such as those relating to earth movement and water damage. You may obtain some relief from the earth movement exclusion by buying the appropriate rider, which is widely available. However, you may experience more difficulty as you seek to reduce exposure to water damage and flood. Commercial insurance companies have not been able to provide flood insurance profitably since people who live on mountains won't buy it, and those who live in river valleys and lowlands always buy it. As a result, the Federal government has a federally-subsidized program for flood insurance. There is some limitation to the Federal protection. It will not, for instance, replace an elaborate basement recreation room.

Residental Worker's Compensation

Another confusing aspect of homeowner's insurance is the requirement, in some states, for worker's compensation coverage if you hire domestic help or other occasional workers to do household chores for you. You may be liable, in your state, so it is wise to be prepared for the problem.

11

AUTOMOBILE INSURANCE

More than 39 states have laws that require the registered owners of vehicles to have insurance. Many other states have financial responsibility laws that allow for the revocation of your license and registration unless you can demonstrate your ability to pay any judgments that may result from an accident. In short, if you drive, you must buy auto insurance.

Who Is Covered?

You, your spouse who is a resident in your household, other family members related by blood, marriage or adoption, including a ward or foster child who is a resident in your household, and who reasonably believe that they are entitled to use one of your vehicles, are covered persons. Anyone who is going to operate a motor vehicle must be protected to the maximum extent possible against such losses.

Medical Payment

The medical payments provision is a special form of accident insurance which provides coverage for medical expenses incurred by insured persons in automobile accidents. It is designed to pay reasonable expenses incurred for necessary medical and funeral expenses due to bodily injury caused by an accident and sustained by a covered person. There are limits to the amount of money that will be paid and to the amount of time that can elapse after the accident occurs.

Vehicle insurance applies to the named insured who suffers bodily injury caused by an accident while occupying a covered automobile. Additionally, people other than the named insured and family members are covered for medical payments while occupying your covered auto. The coverage will also apply to you and your family members if, while you are pedestrians, you are struck by a motor vehicle designed for use on the public roads, or by a trailer of any type.

There are a number of circumstances that will prevent your being covered by this provision. You will not be covered for vehicles with less than four wheels. You will not be covered in automobiles that are used for carrying people or property for a fee, of if you are injured in your employer-provided vehicle. You will also not be covered in an auto that you are operating without being entitled to do so. If you and your family are already covered by some form of health insurance, the medical payments auto coverage is redundant and will only pay the portion of your medical expenses that is not covered by your individual health insurance policy.

Collision Coverage

Collision coverage is to indemnify you against losses caused by the upset of your covered auto, or its collision with another object. This coverage is provided regardless of who is at fault in the accident, and will apply when you cannot recover damages from the party whose negligence caused your loss. This provision makes sure that you can get your vehicle back in operation as quickly as possible.

Comprehensive Coverage

If you sustain a loss that was not caused by the upset of your vehicle, or its collision with another object, you will be reimbursed under the comprehensive section of your policy. This section of your policy covers occurrences such as broken glass, losses caused by missiles or flying objects, fire, theft, larceny, explosion, earthquake, windstorm, hail, water, flood, malicious mischief or vandalism, a riot or civil commotion, or contact with a bird or animal.

There are some exclusions, though, under comprehensive. If you have a CB or audio and video equipment within your vehicle, they can only be protected if you have an additional rider that covers them.

The amount that you can expect your insurer to pay for physical damage to your vehicle will either be the actual cash value of the damaged or stolen property, meaning its replacement value less an allowance for depreciation, or the amount required to repair or replace the property.

Uninsured/Underinsured Motorist Coverage

In spite of mandatory insurance in some 39 states and financial responsibility regulations in practically all states, people still drive motor vehicles without insurance. You can be reasonably certain that a person who drives a motor vehicle without insurance is also a person without resources. The purpose of the uninsured/underinsured provision is to provide protection for you in case you are involved in an accident with someone of this status. At the time of this writing there are 24 states plus the District of Columbia that require this coverage.

No Fault

You might be a resident in one of the 17 states plus Puerto Rico that require no-fault coverage to some degree. The personal auto policies issued in such states will be in compliance with the state regulations. Your policy should be flexible in its provisions, since you may not be involved in an accident in your own state.

The concept of no fault is to save money by not having to go through the process of determining who is to blame. The conventional means of indemnification, which necessitates determining who is at fault and who pays, takes time and also may involve substantial legal fees. No fault, in its pure form, means that it is irrelevant who caused the accident that resulted in bodily injury. The insured party, suffering the loss, would seek recovery for medical expenses, loss of income, and other expenses from his or her own insurer, and there would be no claim for general damages or suffering.

Modified no fault provides limited immunity from the requirement to establish blame in the event of an automobile accident. Under modified no fault, a certain amount of expense will be indemnified under first-party coverage; that is, your own policy will reimburse you regardless of fault. Beyond that limited amount, liability would be determined and you would seek recovery from the party at fault. A modified no fault that expands the first-person coverage limit also exists. With these policies, the injury claims against the individual are indemnified by their company but the company reserves the right to sue the negligent driver's insurance company to recover the amount paid to its insured who was not at fault.

Who Is Insured?

Your personal auto policy covers you, or any family member, while using any auto or trailer. "You," in this case, refers to the named insured listed on the declarations page of the insurance policy and his or her spouse if a resident in the same household. "Family member" refers to a person related to the named insured by blood, marriage, or adoption, including a ward or foster child who is a resident of the named insured's household. The term "resident" has a special legal connotation and may extend beyond the confines of the insured's dwelling. A son or daughter away at school or in the military may still be considered a resident of the household as long as the household is considered "home," and there is an intent to return to the household. Although the covered person definition does not make reference to a requirement or permission, the policy normally will exclude coverage of anyone operating a vehicle without a reasonable belief that he or she is entitled to do so. Also note that the coverage applies to the operation of both the covered vehicle and non-owned vehicles that you or a family member may operate.

Which Vehicles Are Covered?

Any vehicle that is shown on the declarations page is covered. In addition to those, you will be insured for any vehicle for which you acquire ownership during the policy period, provided you ask the insurance company to insure it within 30 days of becoming the owner. This applies to private passenger cars, and also, as long as they are not used in business, pick-ups, panel trucks, and vans. Also covered is any trailer that you might own, and any non-owned auto or trailer being used as a temporary substitute for any vehicle you own which is out of normal use because of breakdown, repair, service, loss, or destruction.

Rental cars are covered by your existing policy, but you may want to secure the collision damage waiver on short-term rentals in order to eliminate your liability for the deductible or any uninsured losses to which the rental car agency is exposed. You should note that some credit card agencies will assume liability, if you rent the car with their credit card.

Other vehicles such as motorcycles, mopeds, all-terrain vehicles, snowmobiles, and other miscellaneous vehicles that you own are covered by your policy if you have secured a miscellaneous vehicle endorsement provision. This provision does not cover rented vehicles of this type.

Insurance For The High-Risk Driver

When you apply for auto insurance, you are evaluated for risk. If you have a driving record with some accidents or violations on it, or if you simply haven't been driving or have never been insured before, the company may turn you down. However, because auto insurance is mandatory, a system had to be devised to cover these drivers. This kind of insurance is called non-standard, shared market, or assigned risk. With these plans, insurance is provided to people who have trouble getting auto insurance from any one company. The shared-market policy costs more than a conventional policy. Any driver with such a policy who has additional traffic violations will suffer stiff and immediate penalties in the form of higher premiums from the insurance company.

If you are a designated high-risk driver and you drive for three years without any traffic violations, you may apply for conventional auto insurance.

STATES WITH UNINSURED MOTORIST COVERAGE REQUIREMENTS

Alaska	New York
Arizona	North Dakota
Connecticut	Oregon
Delaware	Rhode Island
Illinois	South Carolina
Kansas	South Dakota
Maine	Vermont
Maryland	Virginia
Massachusetts	Washington
Minnesota	West Virginia
Missouri	Wisconsin
New Hampshire	Wyoming
New Jersey	Washington, D.C.

STATES WITH NO-FAULT INSURANCE REQUIREMENTS

Colorado	Massachusetts
Connecticut	Michigan
Delaware	Minnesota
Florida	New Jersey
Georgia	New York
Hawaii	North Dakota
Kansas	Oregon
Kentucky	Pennsylvania
Maryland	Utah

Puerto Rico

12

LIABILITY INSURANCE

We all face the risk that our behavior could result in injury to another person or damage to someone's property. We are responsible for the results of our behavior. What is unique about liability insurance is that it has no maximum predictable limit. If you've read or heard about large liability suits, you've probably thought about what would happen if you were the subject of such a suit. If a judgment was won against you, the claimant could take everything you own in addition to whatever insurance you might have. Neither you, your spouse, nor your family members can be expected to behave as reasonable and prudent individuals at all times. We will all, at times, be negligent. If, as a result of one instance of negligence, someone else is subject to a loss as a result of your negligent act, you can expect to be sued and you can expect that the courts will hold in favor of the claimant. To be negligent doesn't mean that you are a bad person; it merely means that you failed to exercise the proper degree of care required under a certain set of circumstances.

Once negligence has been determined, there must be

actual damage or loss as a result of the negligence. In most
cases this is measured by the actual monetary loss suffered
by the injured party. When one suffers a bodily injury as a
result of negligence of another, one may sue for compensatory payments and for specific damages, such as medical
expenses and loss of income. These are relatively easy to
measure. In addition to these specific damages, the injured
party may also ask for general damages to compensate for
the intangible losses resulting from pain and suffering,
disfigurement, mental anguish, and loss of consortium.
The monetary value of these losses is difficult to measure
and, often, very high. Punitive damages, the third form of
damages that may be assessed against the negligent
parties, are a form of punishment. An injury to a party
which results from gross negligence or willful intent is
likely to result in sustainable claims for all three types:
specific damages, general damages, and punitive damages.

The bottom line is that we all need substantial
liability insurance, and we all need to know when such
insurance will not protect us.

When Insurance Won't Help

Liability insurance coverage is not likely to assist us if
our behavior, which is deemed to be negligent, occurred
while we were breaking the law — committing a criminal
or a public wrong. We cannot expect insurance companies
to come to our aid if we commit intentional acts to harm
others. Your personal policy will not cover bodily injury or
property damage arising out of a business pursuit of any
kind, for any insured. Business pursuit liability insurance
needs immediate, proper handling by a qualified property
casualty insurance agent.

Comprehensive Personal Liability Insurance Policy

Comprehensive personal liability coverage can be
acquired as a separate policy or, by adding a rider onto

your individual homeowner policy at the time of purchase. You should consult your property casualty insurance professional to find out which option is most suitable for your circumstances.

Under this type of policy, the company will pay, up to the limits of liability set in the policy, all payments that become the insured's legal obligation because of bodily or property damage falling within the scope of the coverage provided by the policy. In addition, it will pay the legal expenses and attorney's fees for the insurance company's chosen counsel. In addition to the expenses, the contract will pay the interest on judgments plus certain other legal costs. The insurance company has the right to settle a claim or suit against you that it decides is appropriate.

The insureds under your comprehensive liability policy are you, your relatives who are residents of your household, and any other person under age 21 who is in the care of a resident of the household. Comprehensive personal liability policies are useful for people who own condominiums and may be liable for judgments against the condominium association.

Umbrella Liability Policy

The personal umbrella liability policy increases the coverage that home and auto owners normally have within their respective policies. It is a broad-form of liability protection that is purchased in addition to basic insurance. It was originally developed for business purposes and, at one time, was exclusively underwritten by Lloyds of London.

The umbrella policy serves two separate functions. First, it expands your basic coverage since it will pay in excess of the basic coverage amount should it prove to be insufficient. For example, if you have $500,000 of coverage under your basic policy and a $1 million umbrella policy, your total indemnification, for any one liability claim, would be $1.5 million.

The second function of your umbrella liability is to establish broader coverage than that provided under the basic contracts. You should ask your insurer how their company's umbrella policy works. It is desirable that your umbrella liability policy will expand your protection in the areas of slander, defamation of character, invasion of privacy, and damages caused by use of non-owned property in your care, custody, and control.

PART FIVE
OTHER ISSUES

13

MAKING A CLAIM

The first thing you should do when you have a claim is contact your insurance agent or company. In fact, most policies require that you notify your insurer or agent, immediately, if you have a property loss that you think is covered. Your insurer will tell you if you are covered.

If your loss is covered, the next step would be to send a written notice explaining what happened and the nature of the damage. Later, the company may ask you to submit a sworn statement with such particulars as an inventory of personal articles that were lost and estimates for repairs.

Always report any burglary or theft to the local police as well as to your insurance company, and report any loss involving a credit card to the firm that issued the card. If you fail to do either it could invalidate your coverage. Ask questions and get any needed advice from your insurance representative. Make temporary repairs and take any other necessary steps to protect your property from further damage. Save receipts for what you spend and submit them to your insurance company for reimbursement.

Obtain estimates covering repairs to structural damage. Prepare an inventory of lost or damaged personal articles. Include a description of each item, along with its present value, and what you figure to be the dollar amount of the loss. Attach bills, receipts, and other documents that substantiate your figures.

Keep records, including receipts, of any additional living expenses you incur if you have to find other accommodations while your house is being repaired.

Your company will probably assign an adjuster to verify your claim and determine the amount of the loss. Most claims are settled promptly, but some require prolonged investigation, often due to the extent of the loss, or because its cause is unclear.

Arbitrators

Insurance companies recognize that their adjusters and their policyholders don't always see eye to eye on the proper sum for a settlement. The insured does not have to accept an amount he thinks is unfair. If an agreement can't be reached, either party can demand that the dispute be submitted to arbitration. Each party hires its own arbitrator. The two designated arbitrators select a third disinterested arbitrator, whose fee is split between you and your insurer. Whatever amount any two of the arbitrators agree on is considered to be binding.

Liability Situations

You should, immediately, report by phone and in writing any occurrence where you think you are liable. If a neighbor is injured on your property and files a claim against you, you should forward all notices, papers, and other documents to your insurance company as soon as you receive them. Keep copies of everything you send to your insurance company.

Auto Insurance Claims

If your car is involved in an accident — or damaged in some other way such as by fire, flood, or vandalism — or stolen, you should notify your insurance company promptly. Usually, your first step will be a call to your insurance representative. If you have a claim that's covered by your own policy, the insurance company representative can tell you how to proceed. When your car is damaged, you should file a claim with the insurance company if the estimated cost of repairs exceeds the amount of your deductible. Even if you file a claim with the insurer of the driver who was at fault, you should notify your own company. If you have collision coverage, its terms provide for your insurer to pay for the damages, minus the deductible, and then to seek repayment from the other driver's insurer.

Making A Claim Against Someone Else's Policy

If you're legally liable for someone else's injury under conditions covered by your auto or homeowner policy, your insurer will pick up the tab, up to the policy limits. If you are the injured person, or your property is damaged, in most cases you can file a claim under the other party's insurance policy, whether it is a private or commercial one. To file a claim you would call or write the person or organization responsible for your loss, or their insurance company. The insurance company will respond and send a claims representative and an adjuster to obtain the necessary details. All attempts will be made to settle the claim without going to court.

14

WHAT TO DO WHEN YOU ARE DIVORCED... WHEN THE CHILDREN LEAVE HOME

If you adhere to the recommendation that you re-evaluate your insurance status periodically, preferably annually, should your marital status change or your dependents leave home, you can adjust your insurance portfolio accordingly.

Divorce

What you need to do about insurance in the case of divorce depends on several factors. Were you the one administering the family insurance portfolio? If yes, how has the divorce changed your financial goals? Do you, for example, have an annuity contract that was designed to secure your financial health in retirement? Are you the owner of the family health-insurance policy? Are you required to pay spousal and/or child support? Annuity contracts, and cash-value life insurance policies are part of the family assets and will be disposed of in accordance with your settlement.

Health insurance has to be handled in accordance

with the laws of your home state. There are some states that have laws designed to ensure the continued coverage of a divorced spouse if the policyholder is a member of a group health plan. If it is a private health plan, you'll have to consult with the insurance provider. As indicated in Chapter 7, spousal and/or child support obligations should be factored into your life insurance picture.

If you are not the administrator of your family insurance, you should gather all the information you can about your insurance status. If you were awarded ownership of a cash-value life policy, and your spouse still has access to the policy, its value can be diminished if cash is used. You should also make arrangements to be notified in case your spouse misses a premium payment.

The Children Are Grown

The age of your children is only a factor with regard to your health-insurance policy. Even if they continue to live in your home, once your children reach a certain age and/or graduate from college, they will no longer be insured under your policy. Since these requirements vary, you need to consult your policy or insurer.

The time to begin investigating is when your child reaches the age of 19. Some insurance providers will notify you when the child reaches the age of majority and outline your options. But there are some providers who fail to notify, they simply discontinue coverage. There is usually a transition period where your child can automatically qualify for an individual policy. If that period lapses, your child will have to face a medical examination.

With regard to liability, a child and a spouse are covered as long as they reside in the same home. This also applies to the child that is away at college.

15

HIDDEN INSURANCES

There are several kinds of insurance that are tied to certain standard purchases that increase costs without adding much protection. These are: extended warranties, auto service contracts, credit life, credit disability, and mortgage life.

Extended warranties, sometimes referred to as repair insurance, are sold to people who purchase stereos, televisions, VCRs, and appliances such as washers, dryers, and microwaves. It is estimated that less than 15% of the money collected for extended warranty contracts is ever paid out in repairs. Your ability to collect on an extended warranty is subject to the terms and conditions of the warranty. Invariably, terms and conditions are never spelled out until it's too late. Most extended warranties do not cover normal wear and tear or rough handling, or in the case of a camera or camcorder, dropping the equipment.

Auto service contracts are designed to pay for repair and maintenance needs of your car that are not covered by the manufacturer's warranty, or after the original warranty runs out. Service contracts can be underwritten by the manufacturer or by independent companies. Auto service contracts don't usually cover preventative maintenance, towing, if your car breaks down, or rental expenses while your car is in the shop. If the fee for the contract is added to your car loan, you are paying interest on that fee for the duration of the loan. Most service contracts are indemnity contracts and have a $100 deductible that is charged each time you visit the repair shop. So even if you have a covered claim, you may well end up collecting only a few dollars.

Credit life and disability is usually applied to non-mortgage loans. It is designed to insure that the creditor is paid in the event that the insured dies or is disabled before paying off the loan. This is not a bad idea on the surface. The problem is that the insurance attached to your loan is considerably more expensive than what you can get on your own. This insurance also has as a beneficiary, the lending institution, rather than you or your family. Your financial plan should include coverage for your debts, in the event of your disabilty or death.

Mortgage life is designed to pay your mortgage if you die before paying for your home. This is another good idea that is just too costly. Again, the beneficiary is the financial institution and not your family. The premium from the mortgage company is invariably higher than you would pay for the same insurance purchased from another insurer. Here's an example from Charles Given's *Financial Self-Defense*. A 54 year-old man was sold a $100,000 mortgage life policy at the cost of $1,200 per year. That same man could have purchased a $100,000 level term policy from another insurance underwriter for $250 per year.

16

ASSURANCE ABOUT THE INSURANCE INDUSTRY

The word on the street is that the next big bridge over troubled financial waters is the insurance industry. The insurance industry figures into every major financial disaster in recent memory: the savings and loan crisis, the collapse of junk bonds, and the depressed commercial real estate market.

Equitable Life recently announced that it would convert from a mutual company to a stock company in order to raise much-needed cash to shore up its cash reserve.

A Senate subcommittee, headed by Ohio Senator Howard Metzenbaum, is looking into the activities of the insurance industry. He contends that the industry is showing some of the same warning signs that preceded the collapse of scores of savings and loans. He fears that the state regulatory system is not equipped to detect or prevent a financial disaster that could affect millions of Americans whose pensions, investments, and insurance are tied to the insurance industry.

Michael Albanese, an A.M. Best Company analyst, in

testimony before the Metzenbaum committee, called the dire predictions about the financial health of the insurance industry unsupportable. As you know, Best has been examining the overall financial health of 1500 life/health insurers and 2300 property/casualty firms for nearly a century, and Mr. Albanese, speaking on behalf of the company says that the insurance industry "...is not on the brink of financial crisis analogous to that of the savings and loan industry."

STATE INSURANCE COMMISSIONERS' OFFICES

Alabama
(205) 269-3550

Alaska
(907) 465-2515

Arizona
(602) 255-5400

Arkansas
(501) 371-1325

California
(Los Angeles)
(213) 736-2572
(San Francisco)
(415) 557-9624
(Sacramento)
(916) 322-3555

Colorado
(303) 620-4300

Connecticut
(203) 297-3800

Delaware
(302) 736-4251

**District of
Columbia**
(202) 727-4251

Florida
(904) 488-3440

Georgia
(404) 656-2056

Hawaii
(808) 548-5450

Idaho
(208) 334-2250

Illinois
(Chicago)
(312) 814-2420
(Springfield)
(217) 782-4515

Indiana
(317) 232-2386

Iowa
(515) 281-5705

Kansas
(913) 296-7801

Kentucky
(502) 564-3630

Louisiana
(504) 342-5328

Maine
(207) 582-8707

Maryland
(301) 333-2520

Massachusetts
(617) 727-7189

Michigan
(517) 373-9273

Minnesota
(612) 296-6848

Mississippi
(601) 359-3569

Missouri
(314) 751-2451

Montana
(406) 444-2040

Nebraska
(402) 471-2201

Nevada
(702) 885-4270

New Hampshire
(603) 271-2261

New Jersey
(609) 292-5363

New Mexico
(505) 827-4500

New York
(Albany)
(518) 474-6600
(New York City)
(212) 602-0429

North Carolina
(919) 733-7349

North Dakota
(701) 224-2440

Ohio
(614) 644-2658

Oklahoma
(405) 521-2828

Oregon
(503) 378-4271

Pennsylvania
(717) 787-5173

Rhode Island
(401) 277-2246

South Carolina
(803) 737-6117

South Dakota
(605) 773-3563

Tennessee
(615) 741-2241

Texas
(512) 463-6464

Utah
(801) 530-6400

Vermont
(802) 828-3301

Virginia
(804) 786-3741

Washington
(206) 753-7301

West Virginia
(304) 348-3394

Wisconsin
(608) 266-0102

Wyoming
(307) 777-7401

GLOSSARY

AMERICAN COLLEGE: The accrediting body for the CLU (Chartered Life Underwriter) and ChFC (Chartered Financial Planner) designations. It provides undergraduate, graduate, and continuing education in life insurance and financial services courses on both a residence and correspondence basis. American College is based in Bryn Mawr, Pennsylvania.

ANNUITY: Contract sold by insurance companies that pays a monthly, quarterly, semiannual or annual income benefit for the life of the person or annuitant. The annuitant can never outlive the income from the annuity.

BENEFICIARY: Designation, by the policyholder, of a life insurance policy indicating to whom the proceeds are to be paid upon the insured's death or maturity of an endowment.

BENEFIT: Monetary or in kind sum paid or payable to a recipient for which the insurance company has received premiums.

BEST COMPANY: Officially, the A. M. Best Company of New Jersey. Best is a private industry rating service that monitors the insurance industry.

CASH-VALUE LIFE INSURANCE: Overall expression for non-term life insurance policies. Cash-value life contains mortality and expense costs as term policies do, but has an additional charge that earns the policyholder some cash advantages. Cash-value policies include whole life insurance, variable life insurance, universal life, and universal variable life.

CASUALTY/HEALTH INSURANCE: Broad category for all non-life insurance policies.

CHARTERED FINANCIAL CONSULTANT OR PLANNER (ChFC): A professional designation awarded by the American College or its designate. In addition to professional business experience in financial planning, recipients are required to pass national examinations in insurance, investments, taxation, employee benefit plans, estate planning, accounting, and management. ChFC holders are proficient in personal financial planning. See also *American College*.

CHARTERED LIFE UNDERWRITER (CLU): Professional designation also conferred by the American College similar to ChFC with additional requirements for knowledge of economics. A holder of the CLU certificate is technically proficient to help plan individual life insurance programs.

CLAIM: Request by a policyholder for indemnification by an insurance company for loss incurred from an insured peril.

CO-INSURANCE: The insured's share of a covered loss. In property insurance, the 80% rule requires that the insurer pay 80% of the damages up to the amount insured. In commercial health insurance, the insured and the insurer share in a specified ratio of the covered medical costs. See also *deductible*.

COMPENSATORY DAMAGES: See *Liability, Civil Damages Awards*.

CONVERTIBLE TERM LIFE INSURANCE: Coverage that can be converted into permanent insurance regardless of the insured's physical condition without medical examination.

CREDIT LIFE & DISABILITY INSURANCE: Decreasing term insurance policy, usually applied to non-mortgage loans, that is designed to insure that the creditor is paid in the event that the insured dies or is disabled before paying off the loan.

**DECREASING TERM IN-
SURANCE:** Coverage where
the face amount of a life insurance policy declines by a
specified amount each year
over a period of time. The
premium remains constant.
Also known as mortgage life
insurance.

DEDUCTIBLE: Amount of loss
that insured pays in a
claim—including: 1) Absolute
dollar amount. Amount the
insured must pay before company will pay, up to the limits
of the policy. 2) Time period
amount. Length of time the
insured must wait before any
benefit payments are made
by insurance company. Usually applicable to disability
policies.

DISABILITY INSURANCE:
Health insurance that provides income payments to the
insured wage earner when income is interrupted or ter-
minated because of illness or
accident.

ENDOWMENT INSURANCE:
A life insurance policy where
a policyholder receives the
face value of a policy if the
insured survives the endowment period. If the policyholder does not survive, a beneficiary receives the face value
of the policy.

EXPENSE COSTS: A common
cost included in the computation of an insurance premium
that is based on the insurer's
cost of doing business.

GENERAL DAMAGES: See
*Liability, Civil Damages
Awards*.

**HEALTH MAINTENANCE
ORGANIZATION (HMO):**
A prepaid group health insurance plan which entitles
members to services of participating physicians, hospitals,
and clinics. Members of the
HMO pay a flat periodic fee,
usually deducted from each
paycheck, for an assortment
of medical services.

HIDDEN INSURANCE: Insurances that are attached to
standard purchases that increase the costs of the purchase. Hidden insurances include extended warranties,
auto service contracts, credit
life and disability, and mortgage life insurance.

INDEMNITY: Guaranteed
compensation for an insured
loss.

INSURANCE: Plan that wholly
or partially covers the costs of
health care. There are three
basic plans available: commercial health insurance, pri-

vate non-commercial, and social insurance.

INSURANCE FORUM: A monthly newsletter published by Joseph Belth. Belth is an independent industry observer who publishes a list of insurance companies that have received top ratings from the Best Company for the last ten consecutive years.

LIABILITY: The legal obligation to perform or not perform specified acts.

LIABILITY, CIVIL DAMAGES AWARDS: Three types of damages can be awarded to a plaintiff:

1. **Compensatory Damages**—reimbursement for out-of-pocket expenses, including medical bills, legal charges, cost of repairing damaged or destroyed property, and loss of current and projected income. -
2. **General Damages**—reimbursement for damages which do not readily lend themselves to quantitative measurement, commonly known as "pain and suffering."
3. **Punitive Damages**—reimbursement for damages due to gross negligence by a defendant.

LICENSED INSURANCE ADVISER (LIA): License granting legal authority to conduct insurance business in a particular state. In many states, agents and brokers must pass a written exam as a prerequisite to being licensed. The license is usually issued for one or two year periods, and then must renewed.

LIFE INSURANCE: Protection against the death of an individual in the form of payment to a beneficiary—usually a family member, business, or institution. In exchange for a series of premium payments or a single premium payment, upon the death of an insured, the face value and any additional coverage attached to a policy, minus outstanding policy loans and interest, is paid to the beneficiary.

LLOYD'S OF LONDON: Insurance facility composed of many different syndicates, each specializing in a particular risk. Membership in a syndicate is limited to individuals with a large personal net worth, and each member may belong to one or more syndicates depending upon their net worth. Much of the publicity that Lloyd's receives involves insuring exotic risks such as an actress's legs; this represents only a small portion of its total business.

McCARRAN-FERGURSON ACT: The 1945 Federal legislation in which Congress declared that the states may continue to regulate the insurance industry.

MEDICAID: A needs-based medical assistance program financed jointly by Federal and state governments, for the aged, blind, disabled, and families with dependent children.

MEDICARE: A health insurance program paid for, in part, by specified income tax deductions. Medicare is organized in two parts. Part A covers hospitalization costs. Part B is a voluntary component that covers physician services.

MEDIGAP: Medical supplement insurance sold by private insurers to cover the coinsurance of deductible health costs not covered by Medicare.

MORTGAGE LIFE: See *Decreasing Term Life Insurance.*

MORTALITY COSTS: One of common charges included in the computation of a life insurance premium. Mortality costs are based on the life expectancy of the group that the policyholder falls under.

MUTUAL INSURANCE COMPANIES: Companies owned by its policyholders. Many major life insurers are mutual companies.

NEGLIGENCE: Failure to act with the legally required degree of care for others, resulting in harm to them.

NO-FAULT AUTOMOBILE INSURANCE: Type of coverage in which an insured's own policy provides indemnity for bodily injury and/or property damage without regard to fault.

POLICY: Contract or written agreement which puts insurance coverage into effect.

POLICYHOLDER: Person who pays premiums and is covered by the terms of the insurance contract. Also referred to as the insured or policy owner.

PORTFOLIO: The total package of policies underwritten by any given insurance company.

PRE-EXISTING CONDITION: Illnesses or disability for which the policyholder was treated or advised, within a stipulated time period, before applying for a life or health insurance policy.

PREMIUMS: Rate the insured is charged by the insurer for his or her expected loss or risk.

PUNITIVE DAMAGES: See *Liability, Civil Damages Awards.*

RENEWABLE TERM LIFE INSURANCE: Term life insurance coverage that can be renewed, at the option of the insured, without having to take a medical examination.

RIDERS: Additions to an insurance policy that modifies clauses and provisions of the policy, adding or excluding coverage.

SELF-INSURANCE: Protecting against loss by setting aside one's own money.

SHARED RISK PROGRAM: An insurance program for drivers whose history makes them ineligible for conventional automobile insurance.

SOCIAL INSURANCE: A mandatory employee benefit plan under which participants are entitled to a series of benefits as a matter of right. The plan is administered by a Federal or state government agency and is designed to provide a minimum standard of living for those in lower and middle income groups. See also *Social Security.*

SOCIAL SECURITY: A series of government sponsored social insurance programs that include retirement benefits, disability benefits, public assistance, workmen's compensation, food stamps, medicare, and medicaid.

STOCK INSURANCE COMPANIES: Insurance companies that are owned by stockholders. Many leading property/casualty and multi-line insurers are stock insurance companies.

TERM LIFE INSURANCE: Life insurance which stays in effect for a specified, limited period. If an insured dies within that period, the beneficiary receives the death payments. If the insured survives, the policy ends and the beneficiary receives nothing.

See also *Life Insurance* and *Renewable Term Life Insurance*.

UNDERINSURANCE: Failure to maintain adequate coverage for a specific loss or damage.

UNDERINSURED MOTORIST COVERAGE: Addition to a personal automobile policy that covers an insured who is involved in a collision with a driver who does not have sufficient liability insurance to pay for the damages.

UNINSURED MOTORIST COVERAGE: Endorsement to an automobile policy that covers an insured involved in a collision with a driver who does not have liability insurance.

WAIVER OF PREMIUM RIDER: A rider that allows a policyholder with total disability, that lasts for a specified period, to discontinue premium payments for the duration of the disability.

GERALD GLADNEY was an editor at Doubleday & Company and Scholastic Inc. He is a free-lance journalist who has written for various business newsletters and publications.

INDEX